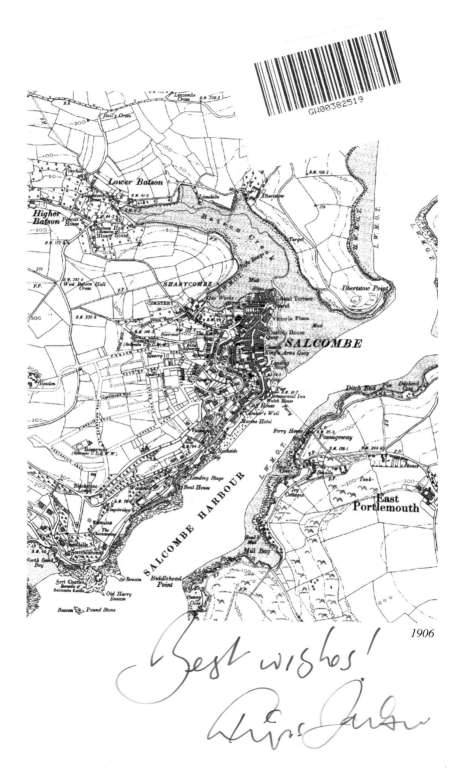

1906

Best wishes!

Around & About

SALCOMBE

Chips Barber

S unny Salcombe, the southernmost town in Devon, is a world-famous sailing centre. Set in an area of unspoilt natural beauty, it is surrounded by green rolling hills, which drop steeply down to its magnificent estuary. Nearby are enormous and spectacular sea cliffs: a natural sheltered harbour with safe sandy coves, it is a Devonshire paradise. But there are those who came here in the past who may not have shared this opinion… Four hundred years ago Salcombe was very different to the resort we see today; a report of the Quarter Sessions in 1607 singled it out as being "full of dissolute seafaring men, who murdered each other and buried them in the sands by night"!

However, Salcombe men united when under threat, proving their loyalty to the King. As the English Civil War (1642–1646) culminated, the Parliamentary forces were mopping up the last vestiges of resistance. Few of their leaders would have considered Fort Charles much of an obstacle. But they were wrong…

The little fort had begun the war as a ruin, but an investment of 'serious money' had made it resilient enough to withstand a prolonged attack. A great deal had also been spent on the fort's arsenal and it was well stocked with provisions. Spoiling tactics by Sir Edmund Fortescue, in charge of the fort, meant the siege was a long one: the defenders were prepared to go the distance and no amount of pressure could persuade them otherwise. The attackers even had to contend with the two Salcombe Castle laundresses, Mary Brown and Elizabeth Terry.

Sir Thomas Fairfax was frustrated at not being able to capture this stronghold. For four months the Roundheads plotted; they then attacked from their headquarters on Rickham Common, on the far bank of the estuary. Despite the use of much ammunition, only two men were killed – one on each side: Samuel Stodard was the unlucky Royalist, whilst Philip Hingston was hit by a pot-shot as he attacked the fort. Sir Edmund was almost a casualty: after he had retired one night, a bullet ricocheted off a wall and hit a leg… on his bed!

Eventually both sides agreed an honourable compromise. Ten conditions of surrender were accepted and the men were allowed to walk out, with their flag held high, to Fallapit, north of Kingsbridge, Sir Edmund's home. Here they disbanded.

The small fort had been a thorn in the side of the Parliamentary forces, so it was no surprise when Colonel Wheldon had it dismantled. Sir Edmund wisely decided not to stay in England; he went to Holland and kept the 16-inch key to the castle as a souvenir.

The town resumed its maritime activities, slowly building up trade in both fishing and – the more important of the two – shipbuilding. An unusual industry of the town was the dredging of sand, from a point close to the dreaded bar. Around 1776–77, as many as 32 barges collected sand to be used as fertiliser on fields in the area.

By 1791 there were 50 properties in Salcombe, housing about 300 people in total. The little port was growing apace and ten years later, at the turn of the century, the population had risen to about 500.

At about that time, the fighting spirit of Salcombe men was aroused again when a French brig got into trouble by running aground on the sunken rock known as The Rickham. Men armed with cutlasses went after the vessel, which they captured and took back to Salcombe as a trophy of war. In recognition of their efforts, each was given a monetary reward.

At the start of the Victorian era, Salcombe possessed the right credentials for prosperity: proximity to the sea; a wonderfully sheltered location; and the availability of natural resources.

Timber was an all-important commodity at that time, and the area was fortunate in being blessed with woodlands, conveniently located near the 'many-fingered' estuary. When better quality timber was required, it was either imported from Canada or taken from large oak woods in the vicinity of Kingsbridge. However, the transportation of timber down to Salcombe was a tough and dangerous task. In 1837 a report in the *Salcombe Times* stated that four local men drowned during a blizzard when their small craft, which was towing a flotilla of timber, was capsized by the strong easterly wind. Their bodies were recovered from the mud at low tide. Two thousand mourners attended the joint funerals of John Harris, John Putt, Thomas Luckham and James March.

The name Sawyer, which is common in the area, derives from the trade of sawing timber in specially-constructed pits. The planks were then placed into the 'steaming box', a device to make them pliable. Prepared to the demands of the craftsmen, ships were built with skill and launched with pride!

Not every launch went smoothly, though. The *Lady Agnes* showed a certain reluctance to enter the water. The problem lay with the greasy slip that she was supposed to slide down – it simply wasn't greasy enough, so boys were sent to run around local houses to scrounge candles. Eventually the slipway did its job and the *Lady Agnes* slid gracefully down into the water in a fashion becoming to her title.

In 1860, it was estimated that 150 vessels could be accommodated at Salcombe, in water that ranged in depth from four to seven fathoms. Boats up to about 70 tons could then proceed easily to Kingsbridge.

In the mid-19th century, four shipyards competed for any available work. Their speciality was the Salcombe clipper, a fast ship which, if handled properly, could reach destinations quickly and transport cargoes at a pace to please merchants. With ships being built ranging between 100 and 550 tons, there was plenty of work for the men. Also at that time, Salcombe had around 1,000 sailors and 25,000 tons of shipping: not surprisingly, its waterfronts were the scene of intense activity.

Fortunately, this quick expansion eventually slowed: had the percentage growth rate continued until the present day, Salcombe would join the ranks of the world's megalopolises!

Salcombe's trading partners included the West Indies, North and South America, and Mediterranean ports, which led to imports of silks from Taranto; ginger from Barbados; rubber from Pará; olive oil from Carloforte; raisins from Patras; coffee, cocoa and tobacco from Puerto Rico; molasses and rum from Antigua; lime juice and spices from Dominica; timber, fruit and cotton from the USA; meat, grain, coffee and hides from South America; oranges from the Azores; and wine, velvet, oil and marble from the Mediterranean. Inevitably there were also ships from less exotic locations, such as the grimy coal barges from the Newcastle area, which nestled up beside the Custom House Quay.

A fast Victorian clipper was the ideal ship for a perishable cargo. This is an extract from a book called *Blue Water Ventures* by Captain Ryder, published in the 1930s: *We would sail out with a cargo of coal from Cardiff to the West Indies and then load sugar, fruit and rum. In those ships also oranges would be fetched from St Michael's, Azores, and the voyage home would be kept as secret as possible. In order to get to the London market before it was known that the ship had even reached home waters, she would refrain altogether from signalling passing vessels or shore stations. If there was a risk of being reported, we would often cover our ship's name up with a board. Nevertheless the crew of any craft which passed to leeward of a fruiter laden with pineapples realised the cargo at once. As a bit of an advertisement one of these Salcombe vessels would, on coming up the Thames, display one of the biggest pineapples at the end of her jib-boom. Those were the days of real seamanship, when these handy clever little ships would despise the services of a tug, and come along through the traffic and strong tide under their own sail right up to Fresh Wharf by London Bridge.*

Captain Ryder went on to add that: *With their tall masts, their shapely yards, well-kept hulls and smart canvas, these Salcombe fruiters were beautiful to behold. Spars* [the maritime, not the supermarket type!] *were kept scraped and varnished, and everything was taut and trim from truck to deck. Some of them by their very names indicated pride of origin:* Queen of the West, Queen of the South, Salcombe Castle, Western Belle, Avon, Lord Devon, Malborough, *and* Erme.

But it was not always as romantic as it might sound. There were difficult times in port as well as out on storm-tossed seas.

The person who named a Salcombe-registered vessel 'the *Neptune*' probably thought that here he had a craft able to defy the waves. What he didn't allow for was the ship catching fire. The mate cut her moorings and she drifted ashore, burnt out, then sank. What a waste of nine tons of beer!

So, as we have seen, Salcombe was a busy hive of shipbuilding, with the unmistakable sound of the caulking mallet, the smell of pitch and tar – indeed a golden age. The work went on apace with the allied trades of rope and sail-making, smiths and suppliers all enjoying a boom time. But it wasn't to last…

About a century ago, this appeared in *Kelly's Directory* for Devon: *Salcombe is a sub-port of Dartmouth and the chief port of the Kingsbridge district and has its own registration of shipping, a custom house, and coastguard station. The harbour, although capable of receiving vessels of a large tonnage, is better adapted for ships of average size, owing to the narrowness and the intricacies of navigation which are presented by large rocks which lie at the entrance. The climate of this district is very mild; the American aloe blooms in the open air and oranges, lemons and citrons reach a state of ripe perfection, and in this circumstance, combined with the beauty of the surrounding scenery, has of late brought it into favour as a watering place.*

This most southerly of Devonshire towns was remote in Victorian times. The main contact with the rest of the world was through the steamer, the *Kingsbridge Packet*. It plied up and down the estuary daily, extending the journey to Plymouth twice weekly.

Salcombe

In the mid-19th century, the obvious way to get to Kingsbridge was by water. Rowing boats were used at first and competition for passengers was keen between the various muscle-bound ferrymen. While Mr March of Union Street, Salcombe usually had his fair share of male passengers, he just could not compete with Edward Woods for the female trade: the latter was so handsome that young ladies went to Kingsbridge just to gaze upon him! However, once steamers replaced rowing boats, Mr March remained in the business of conveying passengers to Kingsbridge, whilst no further mention was made of the dashing Edward Woods!

In 1894, one traveller who arrived in Salcombe by road recorded his first-hand experience of the tribulations of his less than comfortable journey: ... *I at last decided to visit Salcombe. I went to Kingsbridge by train and proceeded thence by what, for courtesy's sake, is called a 'coach'. This consisted of a rattletrap box on wheels which would be a disgrace to any place. I am told that an improvement in this direction will be made. Squeezed, jolted and cross, I and my friend arrived at the Marine Hotel.*

The *Western Morning News* included these observations in early July 1896: [it is] *not so many years since Salcombe was scarcely known to the outside world. It is not by any means 'discovered' yet. There was one thing which tended to keep its existence in the memory of a few. This was shipbuilding. Yes. One would scarcely imagine such a peaceful old spot and old-world-looking village had once earned itself a famous name for its wooden clippers, many of which eventually found their way to the Mediterranean. The whole settlement today suggests an out-of-the-way fishing village. Singularly enough this has never formed part of the industry of the place. Fishing there is, yet only of a desultory character. But little – scarcely anything, indeed – remains of the shipbuilding industry. The advent of steam and iron ships killed it and the prospects of Salcombe at one and the same time. Time was when the old-fashioned houses of Salcombe proper, with its little narrow streets and passages, were filled with master mariners and sailors of the mercantile marine. But the collapse of shipbuilding drove them away. Salcombe, to put it popularly, appeared to be 'going to the dogs' as far as the town was concerned. Houses remained unoccupied and fell into disrepair. To stop the rot alternatives were discussed and serious thought was given to the idea of building iron ships, Snapes Point being the favoured location for such a venture. It was only when the economics of such an enterprise were given close consideration that it was realised that Salcombe would never be able to compete as the raw materials were too far away and too expensive to haul to the southernmost tip of Devon. Thus the thriving little port of Salcombe became a ghost town and the population dwindled as men left it in search of work elsewhere.*

For years the place remained 'undiscovered' – unthought of by the energetic tourist. Its potential, however, was recognised by Dr John Huxham, an eminent Plymouth physician. He saw enough similarities in both the landscape and climate to proclaim Salcombe 'The Montpellier of England!'

At length the horizon cleared. The Earl of Devon's estate above the old town – stretching out to Bolt Head – one day came onto the market. A company was formed in London, and it at once purchased eighty-eight acres of land near the town. The directors of the South Devon Land Company saw their opportunity. What is perhaps better, they seized it. To employ a modern colloquialism, they began to 'boom' Salcombe. This was the only remedy for the decay and neglect of so charming a spot.

The article went on to recommend that the development should continue in a cautious fashion, as the construction of properties that would never be occupied could be a waste of time. However, the author was optimistic that Salcombe did have a future and thus added: Salcombe will, at no very distant date, develop into what Nature has most fitted it for. It will be a second Torquay – perhaps 'The Princess of Watering Places' [Torquay being the Queen!] for no-one wants to depose Torquay.

Evidence of the state of the main road to Salcombe comes from the fact that most of the materials needed to build new houses came by boat, the easiest and most economic way to get anything to Salcombe.

Intrinsic to the development of Victorian towns was the influence of the railways. Salcombe was an outpost: the nearest station was more than four miles away. It was not an impossible task to link it to the rail network, but was it desirable? The Great Western Railway took five years considering whether to link these two places. It gave people time to weigh up objectively the pros and cons, whilst also giving the railway company time to assess the success of the Kingsbridge branch.

The late Raymond B. Cattell was a world-famous psychologist who wrote of his journey along the coast and overland in South Devon in *Under Sail Through Red Devon*, first published in 1937. He commented: *Many years ago, Salcombe decided by a majority vote that it didn't want the railway. Elsewhere the shop and hotel-keepers by sheer numbers might have defeated such a resolution; for in some places no moral odium attaches to putting bank balances before the beauty and integrity of the homeland. But these were wiser men and their policy of seclusion has justified itself right up to the hilt.*

The line was never built. Salcombe didn't become 'The Princess of Watering Places' and there were many residents who celebrated!

The more discerning (and affluent) types spread the word regarding the delights of this select place; large, grand houses started springing up on the hillsides in the best positions to get a glimpse of the estuary.

This influx of wealthy people continued through the 1920s. In 1928, Otto Christop Jos Gerrard Ludwig Overbeck acquired a lovely house called Sharpitor. He was an inventor who created the first machine for vibro massage. As a great believer in the use of electricity to deal with medical problems, he experimented on himself and others. At the age of 40 he was bald; through experimentation, he reputedly regained a full head of hair by the time he was 60! Not all his experiments were so successful, however. Attempts to pass an electric current through a bed on which he was lying led him to a spell of 18 months in hospital!

Overbeck believed that the application of science would enable people to live to be 350 years old, and was keen to lead by example. Unfortunately, he fell short of this target

by 265 years, in 1937! He bequeathed his land and various possessions to groups which he felt would most benefit. He wanted his house to be used as a youth hostel, so gave the property to the National Trust on condition that it be used for this purpose.

Also for the National Trust, at a ceremony at Bolt Head in June 1928, Mr Stenton Covington accepted 600 acres of land from the Earl of Devon. It included coastline on both sides of the estuary, extending from the vicinity of Gara Rock up the Salcombe estuary to Mill Bay, and from the Courtenay Walk at Sharpitor through Bolt Head, on to Soar Mill Cove. At the time, the funds did not extend to acquiring all the coast as far as Bolt Tail: that came later!

As we have seen, Salcombe enjoys a reputation for being as close to 'paradise' as it is possible to get on these shores. The enjoyment of this idyll by one particular man, however, was interrupted in July 1937 by a 'monstrous' scare. While Sidney Field of Salcombe was on the estuary, surveying the surroundings, he suddenly noticed the water break near him to reveal a large oval-shaped head with big bulging eyes, protruding a foot or more above the surface. Stretching for 20 feet behind the head was an eel-like body, which occasionally flicked a large scaly tail out of the water as the creature swam around. Sidney was mesmerised by this strange creature, and it was a minute or two before it occurred to him to fetch another witness. By the time he had found someone, the creature had gone! Fortunately many people believed him, for two good reasons: firstly, this was a man who had sailed in foreign waters and was accustomed to sighting unusual, but identifiable, animals; secondly, a few weeks earlier, at Redlap Cove near Dartmouth, the head gardener of the estate on the cliffs had seen a similar sight. Natural historians, however, failed to identify the monster. Perhaps Salcombe has its own 'Nessie' – what a potential boon for the tourist trade!

Alfred, Lord Tennyson succeeded William Wordsworth as Poet Laureate in 1850. It has been said that the majestic, musical language of the *Lotus Eaters* (1832) was inspired by the atmosphere of Salcombe and its environs. He was an old and ailing man by the time he wrote *Crossing the Bar* – a favourite at funerals – which is said to be based on the difficult journey out of the mouth of the Salcombe estuary. He was created a peer in 1883 and became the first Baron Tennyson, a title he held until his death in 1892, at the age of 83.

Professor Cattell featured a few chapters on Salcombe and its estuary in *Under Sail Through Red Devon*: *On either side the little bays and golden sands of Salcombe beckon. Where is there sand of a lovelier, livelier hue than this? Wondrously they beckon to the sea-weary mariner and to add glamour to their call they are sprinkled in summer with sprawling sirens in many-coloured bathing costumes.*

Through the limpid pale green waters we can clearly see the yellow sand of the bar, eight feet, six feet, and now four feet beneath our keel. As it shallows we see the rocky islands, marked by lantern poles – the molars which grind the victims caught by the fangs of the bar. For though we drift languidly now, lulled to the languor by the pleasant sights and sounds, Salcombe can present a very different aspect to the sailor. I have seen the beauty of its other face in winter, when the gale thunders harshly through the dripping, straining pine woods and howls furiously against the black buttresses of Bolt Head. Then the bar is a deathtrap for any homing sailor and all too many have come to grief there. It stretches – a white line of raging waters – from the eastern bank to within a stone's throw of the high western cliff, leaving the narrowest of safe passages, and it may well be called the most dangerous bar on the south coast. Even in summer there are many yachtsmen who will not dare to enter after dark, and since the tide may be unsuitable during the day it is something of a feat to get into Salcombe, a feat which so exhausts some that, once accomplished, they drop anchor and go ashore for the rest of the season!

Cattell also noted: *By some miracle of mercy, Salcombe, in spite of its incomparable natural beauty, has remained one of the few completely unspoilt gems of Devon. Its compact little streets are neat and clean but quaintly old-fashioned, its tasteful villas are in lovely grounds where every kind of tree seems to flourish. If it must spawn characterless terraces it chooses to do so over the hill away from the river.*

And so the years have passed, and Salcombe, 'the Bride of the Sea', has seen further residential growth on its outskirts. The rich and the famous have also used Salcombe as their playground. Many years ago, guests to the Marine Hotel included writer Paul Gallico, and film stars Jack Hawkins and Peter O'Toole. In the 1990s, during one of Salcombe's famous regatta weeks, it was said that there were more cast members of *Coronation Street* in the port than in 'Weatherfield'!

During the last years of his life, James Anthony Froude, the 19th-century Dartington-born historian, lived at Woodcot, a large house in Salcombe. Although his greatest work was the 12-volume *History of England,* most of his writings tended to be based on his many adventures: each of his journeys, to Ireland, New Zealand, Australia, the West Indies and South Africa, became a book! At Salcombe he sailed the sea and explored the countryside. In describing some of his extraordinary activities, one contemporary said, "No horse could throw him and no storm could make him seasick." He was a controversial character, who was often at odds with his religious peers or with other eminent historians, who felt that a lot of his writings were inaccurate, misinterpreted or both! It appears that when Froude had convinced himself that he was right, nothing – not even proven fact – could persuade him to change his views; thus he had many critics. But he was famous in his day for his 'common touch' – the ability to write in a way which appealed to people. He died in 1894 and was buried in Salcombe.

Despite his controversial nature, at least he was never hounded out of his home like a couple of his predecessors were! Many years earlier a young girl had been working for a wealthy couple who resided at Woodcot. Despite protesting her innocence, she was accused of theft, and at 'prayers' one night, when everyone in the large house was assembled, the master and mistress announced that the girl was to be taken into custody the next day. The following morning, however, she was not to be found – and her belongings were still in her room! A few weeks later her badly decomposed body was washed up on the shore, along the coast at Hope Cove. The reaction by Salcombe folk to the unfair way in which the girl had been handled was unanimous – they harassed the couple until they left Salcombe for good!

Long before the days of fibre optics, Salcombe was the chosen spot for the English end of the French-Atlantic telegraph cable, which linked France with London. The first landfall point was Starehole Bottom (28 May 1870), and a house was constructed ready to receive it. However, after weeks of trying, the communications link was deemed unsuitable, so was removed to nearby North Sands. The job was completed here, some 18 months later. The original building constructed to house the machinery is now called Cable Cottage!

The first Salcombe lifeboat (1869) was called the *Rescue*; it was the generous gift of Richard Durant of Sharpham House, Ashprington. The village pub at Ashprington is called The Durant Arms in honour of him, while his house remains conspicuous on the west bank of the Dart Estuary, a short distance from Totnes.

The saddest day in the history of Salcombe's lifeboats was 16 October 1916 when *William and Emma* went to the aid of the *Western Lass,* a Plymouth schooner, which had gone aground at Lannacombe Bay, a few miles east of Salcombe. The crossing of Salcombe's notorious bar was an ordeal for the crew, especially as the autumnal gales had contrived to produce almost impossible sea conditions. As they struggled on through the storm to reach the *Western Lass*, the lifeboatmen were unaware that the crew of the stricken vessel had already been rescued.

Finding the ship deserted, they turned homewards for Salcombe, but disaster – and the cruel hand of irony – struck them near the mouth of the Salcombe estuary. An enormous wave caught the lifeboat in the stern and threw it high into the air. The men were all thrown into a heap on one side of the boat, and became entangled with various bits of equipment. Before they could extricate themselves, another monstrous wave capsized the boat. Only two of the 15 crew, Bill Johnson and Eddie Distin, survived. Eddie Distin demonstrated his remarkable constitution by remaining coxswain for 30 years. Bill Johnson never fully recovered from the ordeal and died a few years later.

The inquest on 3 November 1916 heard why Salcombe had chosen this particular type of boat several years earlier: the non-righting vessel had been selected because it was more spacious and had better sailing qualities than the self-righting boat.

Salcombe's lifeboat is one of the busiest in Britain, and its functions are wide ranging. It has been the subject of a television documentary series, which followed the crew at work. You can read about their exploits if you wait for the ferry to Portlemouth, as details of rescues are recorded there in black and white – literally.

It is hard to imagine Salcombe as a manufacturing centre, but according to experts it produces the best ice-cream in Britain. Americans Herb Wolff and Carol Robbins are the husband and wife team who wrote *The Very Best Ice Cream and Where To Find It*. They sampled some three thousand varieties before proclaiming Salcombe to have the best ice-cream in the UK, an accolade which certainly takes some licking!

East Portlemouth may be small now, but it was quite important once. It has a mention in the *Domesday Book,* and supported a population well in excess of Salcombe's! It was early in the 19th century that it began to decline, when the west bank became the favoured side of the river.

High on that hill is East Portlemouth's church, dedicated to St Winwaloe, a Breton saint who was reputed never to sit down at church services. (This, of course, is likely as very few seats were found in churches at that time!) Locally this saint is also referred to as Onalaus or Onslow (Onslow Road is in Salcombe). The Dowager Duchess and Duke of Cleveland, owners of the manor, funded restoration work carried out here, though it was not to the taste of some: the celebrated Revd Sabine Baring-Gould used the phrase 'barbarously restored' when summing up his uncomplimentary opinion of the work.

Close to the belfry door is a large grave containing the remains of six Frenchmen who were aboard the schooner *Pauline,* which was shipwrecked near the Rickham coast-guard station on 15 October 1877.

Smuggling was once rife in East Portlemouth, until the Duke of Cleveland drew up extreme measures to eliminate the nefarious activities there. He ordered the demolition of the village's two pubs and several houses, so that the smugglers would find it impossible to continue. The village still has no pub today!

The stretch of coastline from Bolt Head to Bolt Tail has seen so many wrecks it has long been regarded as a grave-yard for shipping. Viewed from the sea, it is a huge inhos-pitable wall that seems to attract ships in stormy weather. It has been suggested by captains of ships that have run aground in calm but foggy conditions, that their compasses were affected by the metal content in these cliffs. The theory has so far not been proven but it remains a better excuse than admitting a poor piece of navigation (400-foot cliffs? Where?).

The most publicised shipwreck was that of the *Herzogin Cecilie*, a windjammer of exquisite beauty, and a ship that stole the hearts of all who sailed in her. She was exceptional – a champion of the high seas, and an eight times winner of the unofficial grain race from Australia. Built in Bremerhaven in 1902, she was 334 feet long, and her mainmast stretched some 200 feet towards the heavens. Her design and her 56,000 square feet of sail enabled her to set record after record. At about 3,250 tons she was the largest ship on Lloyd's Register, and management there must have been horrified at the news of her destruction.

In late April 1936, Captain Sven Eriksson was extremely pleased to have completed the journey from Australia to the Cornish port of Falmouth in just 86 days. However, his wife, Pamela Bourne, a well-known author at that time, had a premonition about the next stage of the journey up the English Channel to Ipswich. Her fears were confirmed: the ship ran aground near Sewer Mill Cove (known today as Soar Mill Cove). The crew of 22 left, as did a young lady from Newton Abbot, a friend of the captain's wife. Even the ship's parrot, despite a fair amount of squawking, was brought ashore. The captain stayed aboard as long as he dared. Despite intense salvage attempts, the combination of adverse weather conditions and the way in which she had come to rest militated against an early solution to her plight.

On hearing of the wreck, the public's response was amazing. The *Western Morning News* reported: *There was a queue of motor cars over a mile long yesterday afternoon near the scene of the wreck on Bolt Head of the barque* Herzogin Cecilie, *such are the immediate results of media publicity. Spectators came from all parts of Devon and Cornwall and even further afield and it was reliably estimated that at the peak of the period there were over 1,000 cars and ten thousand people in the vicinity. During the weekend 50,000 people must have viewed the wreck.*

Spacious as are the rock-crowned cliffs, they seemed to be in all places crowded with thrilled onlookers, and every path from all directions was dotted with moving people. Police controlled a difficult situation admirably.

Some went to extraordinary lengths to capture on film the graceful four-masted vessel. The newsreel photographer, John Dored, chartered an aeroplane. He discovered that the best way to capture the most impressive shots was to fly down the face of the cliff, a manoeuvre which scared him witless – several times! The film shot that day was presented to cinema-goers that same night, something highly unusual for the 1930s.

After seven weeks the *Herzogin Cecilie* was hauled to Starehole Bay, near Bolt Head. It was felt that salvage operations would be better effected in a more sheltered spot. What they didn't bargain for was the cussedness of the weather, as the meteorological gremlins went to work. Despite the punishing exertions of the salvage team, a south-easterly gale baulked their utmost efforts and inflicted grave damage to the stricken ship.

There was no hope for her. On 19 January 1939, a brief newspaper report stated that: *Without warning, the famous sailing ship the* Herzogin Cecilie, *which has lain in Starehole Bay at the entrance to Salcombe Harbour since 19 June 1936, capsized and disappeared yesterday. Wreckage is floating up in the harbour and in the channel.*

Much as I hope you enjoy reading of the delights of Salcombe and surrounding area in this book, the very best way to soak up the atmosphere is to get out there. I'm therefore devoting the rest of this short guide to describing two walks that will help you to experience the beauty of the countryside.

South Sands is aptly named because it is the last beach of any note on the west side of the estuary before the open sea. There is a small paying car park at the Tides Reach Hotel. This is opposite and behind the original lifeboat station, which was built in 1877 and used until about 1925. However, if you are based in Salcombe town there is a pleasant ferry ride to South Sands which removes the need to park.

Stout shoes are suggested for this three-mile circular stroll, as there are many places where exposed rocks make underfoot conditions painful for those with thin-soled shoes.

From the former lifeboat station, climb up the steep hill behind it. This is a No Through Road which leads to Sharpitor, and some other expensive properties. The first section is along the road and will help you to get into your stride. Soon a gate to Overbecks is reached; pass through it and head up the drive. After a hundred yards or so, routes split: take the left one, marked 'Bolt Head via Stare Hole Bay'.

Views of the sea will be limited initially, because trees line this pedestrian-only thorough-fare. Soon they thin out and then disappear, providing views south-eastwards along the coast to Prawle Point.

The path, known as the Courtenay Walk, gets stonier and rockier underfoot as it passes through the spectacular surroundings. Stone steps are cut in the rock; a handrail on the seaward side prevents anyone from slipping over the edge.

The path passes beneath Sharp Tor's many grand rock piles and turns to enter Starehole Bay from a lofty access point. Continue onwards to where you encounter a sort of hanging valley, which reaches the coast a short way ahead. This is Starehole Bottom, and if you turn your back to the sea and look up, it bears a striking resemblance to Dartmoor. However, the rock type is very different: not granite, but a metamorphic schist!

A signpost offers a choice of routes, but as Bolt Head is so near, it would be foolish not to make the extra bit of effort needed to scale its dizzy heights.

Nearby, up two flights of eight steps, is the now redundant coastguard lookout. From here a wide expanse of sea can be surveyed. Down Channel, the Eddystone Lighthouse is visible, in the right conditions.

The next point to head for can be seen about 300 yards away, in the shape of a signpost on top of the cliff. As you approach it, the slope becomes far steeper, and the sign temporarily disappears from view. When you reach it, you will probably be impressed at the extent of what you can see, providing you are familiar with the Devonshire topography.

Do not cross the stile. Turn right along the route marked 'Malborough – South Sands – Overbecks'. This path starts off as a grassy level corridor running beside a wall. After a few hundred yards it starts to dip gently and then more steeply. Ignore any routes that cut across your line; descend into Starehole Bottom to cross its stream for the second time today. A stepped slope leads up and out of this valley.

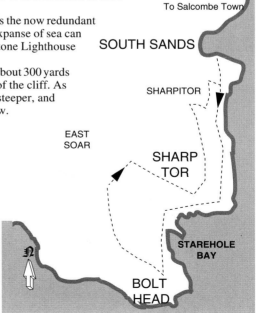

Continue on to 'Sharp Tor – Overbecks'. With the fence on your left, and the steep gully of Starehole Bottom to your right, you will easily reach the top of Sharp Tor. The bollard or capstan is a memorial to W. Newton Drew, a former resident of Ringrone, a large house near Overbecks that we shall pass later. It is a most informative oracle, with a compass and sight lines indicating the direction and distances of familiar places and landmarks.

Once you have had your fill of the view, continue on in the general direction of Salcombe.

After a short time, a redundant trig point appears on the left. From here, Malborough's church spire forms a distinct landmark. In the distance, beyond, it is possible to discern the outline of the china clay workings of Lee Moor on the western fringe of Dartmoor.

The path drops down, and the scrubby vegetation obscures the view of the estuary and Salcombe. At the bottom of a flight of steps, a T-junction is encountered. Turn right and go downhill. The path now twists and turns before reaching Overbecks; the entrance to the property is striking with its exotic tropical vegetation. From here, the way is all downhill, through a woody environment. Stay on the zigzagging surfaced road back to South Sands.

The second walk is an estuary and coastal stroll. If Salcombe is the starting point, it will be necessary to cross by the ferry to the East Portlemouth side of the river. Although this is a journey of only about 200 yards, it saves a road journey of more than 20 miles! The last ferryman to row his customers across was Ferryman Distin, who developed very broad shoulders as his services were in great demand. A motor ferry service was introduced in 1911; it runs every day except Christmas Day.

On reaching the eastern side of the estuary, stroll southwards along the road with its many

'private' signs and privacy-seeking fences. You may catch a glimpse of the very small Small's Cove! Small's House caught fire in 1911 and the Salcombe fire brigade had no choice but to take their horse-drawn fire engine to it on the ferry. The property didn't stand a chance.

Many years ago, it was common to see the beach covered with crab pots. Not so common, though, were the contents... fishermen's wives, busy on the beach, used to pop their tiny tots inside the crab pots – they made ideal playpens!

With that picture in mind, continue onwards until you reach Mill Bay. Here you will see the remains of a concrete slipway. This was built in the Second World War by the United States Naval Constructional Battalion. At this point they repaired landing craft that had been damaged in the D-Day landings.

It is not surprising that many would-be walkers get only as far as the golden sands of Mill Bay. But you are set for greater things. Take the closest footpath to the water (right), not the higher cliff path. Your chosen route is one that rises and falls regularly for the next mile or so.

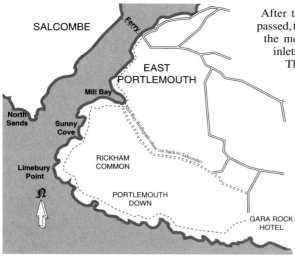

SALCOMBE

EAST
PORTLEMOUTH

Ferry

Mill Bay

North
Sands

Sunny
Cove

Mill Bay Bridlepath (also cut back to Salcombe)

Limebury
Point

RICKHAM
COMMON

PORTLEMOUTH
DOWN

GARA ROCK
HOTEL

After the aptly-named Sunny Cove is passed, there are tremendous views across the mouth of the estuary to the twin inlets of South Sands and North Sands. This section of the South Devon Coastal Footpath is one of the most popular with walkers, but being close to Salcombe (and, by that token, civilisation), many of the people you will pass will be 'casual' walkers, conspicuous by their choice of footwear: this can range from sensible trainers down to open sandals – hardly ideal for this type of terrain! The way ahead is along the winding coast path. Rickham Common, or at least the edge of it, is traversed. There used to be a nine-hole golf course here.

The general trend of the coastal path is upwards. Our destination is the Gara Rock Hotel, which only comes into sight once we are close to it.

The hotel is the ideal location to get refreshments before returning to Salcombe. It started out as the Rickham Coastguard Station in the 1840s. In 1909, it became a guest house, and over the years has evolved into a superb hotel. Many famous people have stayed here over the years, including Sir Laurence Olivier, Margaret Rutherford and Sir John Betjeman, adding another Poet Laureate to the list of those who have enjoyed the poetic views!

Refreshed and relaxed, you now have a choice of routes to return to Salcombe. Those who want a short cut, to save themselves a longer return journey, should walk down the drive of the Gara Rock Hotel. A short distance on, just past the first bend, is a footpath signed to the left. Initially, it will take you across fields and then down a muddy lane to a road. Beyond, the track runs down the narrow valley that leads gently to Mill Bay: all good downhill stuff. However, if your energy reserves permit you to, it is far better to return along the coast path from Gara Rock. The views always look different in the other direction, and, as you enter the Salcombe estuary, you will once more begin to see the reason why so many people fall in love with the southern tip of Devon. Who could blame them? It's an incredible place!

ALSO BY THE AUTHOR

Diary of a Dartmoor Walker • Diary of a Devonshire Walker
The Great Little Dartmoor Book • The Great Little Totnes Book
The Great Little Plymouth Book • Plymouth in Colour
Dark & Dastardly Dartmoor • Weird & Wonderful Dartmoor
Ghastly & Ghostly Devon • Haunted Pubs in Devon
Dartmouth and Kingswear • The South Hams in Colour
Film and TV Programmes…Made in Devon • The Dartmoor Quiz Book
Ten Family Walks on Dartmoor • Six Short Pub Walks on Dartmoor
From The Dart to The Start • Newton Ferrers and Noss Mayo
Around & About Burgh Island and Bigbury Bay
Around & About Hope Cove and Thurlestone
Place Names in Devon • An A–Z of Devon Dialect
Colourful Dartmoor • The Story of Hallsands
Devon's Railways of Yesteryear • Along The Avon
Walk the South Hams Coast–Dartmouth to Salcombe
Walk the South Hams Coast–Salcombe to Plymouth

OTHER TITLES ABOUT THIS AREA

Under Sail Through South Devon & Dartmoor, *Raymond B. Cattell*
Haunted Happenings in Devon, *Judy Chard*
The Ghosts of Berry Pomeroy Castle, *Deryck Seymour*
Walks in the South Hams, *Brian Carter*
The Ghosts of Totnes, *Bob Mann*
The Dartmoor Mountain Bike Guide, *Peter Barnes*
Walks in the Totnes Countryside, *Bob Mann*
Dart Country, *Deryck Seymour*
Murders and Mysteries in Devon, *Ann James*
Circular Walks on Eastern Dartmoor, *Liz Jones*
Dartmoor Letterboxing for Beginners, *Kevin Weall*
Beesands and Hallsands of Yesteryear, *Cyril Courtney*
Beesands and Torcross of Yesteryear, *Cyril Courtney*
Churches of The South Hams, Parts One and Two, *Walter Jacobson*
Villages of The South Hams, *John Legge*

*We have over 180 Devon-based titles; for a list of current books please send SAE to
2 Church Hill, Pinhoe, Exeter, EX4 9ER or telephone 01392 468556*

Plate Acknowledgements:

All photographs are by or belong to Chips Barber

*First published in 1993 (ISBN 0 946651 76 0)
reprinted in 2003 by
Obelisk Publications, 2 Church Hill, Pinhoe, Exeter, Devon
Designed and Typeset by Sally Barber
Printed in Great Britain
by Image Design & Print Ltd, Bodmin, Cornwall*

ISBN: 1 903585 32 5

Price : 1.95